Yorkie Poo as Pets

A Complete Yorkie Poo Owner's Guide

Yorkie Poo Breeding, Where to Buy, Types, Care, Cost, Diet, Grooming, and Training all Included.

By: Lolly Brown

Foreword

Yorkie Poo breeds are considered as one of the most adorable yet confident breed of dogs in the world. These dogs are a hybrid of a Yorkshire Terrier and a Toy Poodle and had been around for over a decade already. They have a reputation of being energetic, obedient and adorable; they are greatly admired as pets because of their confidence and charismatic attitude.

Although Yorkie Poos are truly a great choice as pets, these dogs doesn't come with a thin instruction manual, but fear not! In this book you'll be easily guided on understanding your Yorkie Poo dog, their behaviors, their characteristics, how you should feed and care for them and a whole lot more.

Embark on a wonderful journey of sharing your life with a Yorkie Poo. Learn to maximize the great privilege of living with one and be able to share this unique and unforgettable experience just like many *millenials* that came before you!

Table of Contents

Introduction 1

    Glossary of Dog Terms 3

Chapter One: Yorkie Poo in Focus 9

    Facts About Yorkie Poos 10

        Quick Facts 13

    Yorkie Poo Breed History 14

Chapter Two: Yorkie Poo Requirements 17

    License Requirements 18

        United States Licensing for Dogs 18

        Great Britain Licensing for Dogs 19

    How Many Yorkie Poo Should You Keep? 20

    Do Yorkie Poos Get Along with Other Pets? 21

    Ease and Cost of Care 21

        Initial Costs 22

        Monthly Costs 27

    Pros and Cons of Yorkie Poo 30

Chapter Three: Tips in Buying a Yorkie Poo 33

    Finding a Reputable Yorkie Poo Breeder 34

    Tips in Choosing a Reputable Breeder 34

    Rescue Dogs Adoption 36

    List of Breeders and Rescue Websites 37

U.S. Yorkie Poo Breeders...37

U.S. Yorkie Poo Recues...39

U.K. Yorkie Poo Breeders..39

U.K. Yorkie Poo Rescues 40

Selecting a Healthy Yorkie Poo 40

Tips on How to Puppy-Proof Your Home..........................43

Chapter Four: Caring Guidelines for Yorkie Poos 45

Ideal Habitat Requirements for Yorkie Poos.....................46

Supplies and Equipment for Your Yorkie Poo...................47

Setting Up Your Yorkie Poo's Crate 50

Chapter Five: Nutritional Needs of Yorkie Poo....................51

The Nutritional Needs of Dogs 52

How to Select a Healthy Dog Food Brand 54

Tips for Feeding Your Yorkie Poo.......................................57

Toxic Foods to Avoid 58

Chapter Six: Training Your Yorkie Poo.................................61

Socializing Your Puppy 62

Tips in Training Your Yorkie Poo 64

Tips in Housebreaking Your Yorkie Poo Puppy 66

Chapter Seven: Grooming Your Yorkie Poo 71

Recommended Tools for Grooming 73

Tips for Bathing and Grooming Yorkie Poos.....................74

Other Grooming Tasks 76

Chapter Eight: Breeding Your Yorkie Poo 79

Basic Dog Breeding Information 80

Mating Behavior of Dogs 80

Tips for Breeding Your Yorkie Poo 82

Labor Process of Yorkie Poos 84

Breeding Method used to Produce Yorkie Poos 86

Chapter Nine: Keeping Your Yorkie Poo Healthy 89

Common Health Problems of Yorkie Poos 90

Recommended Vaccinations for Yorkie Poos 106

Signs of Possible Illnesses 108

Yorkie Poo Care Sheet 111

Basic Yorkie Poo Information 112

Habitat Requirements 113

Nutritional Needs 114

Breeding Information 115

Index 117

Photo Credits 125

References 127

Introduction

Yorkie-Poo is a hybrid of a Yorkshire Terrier and a Toy or Miniature Poodle, hence the name. They are also known as Yorkiepoo, Yo-Yopoo or a Yorkiedoodle. These breed was originally developed to create a small-sized dog - free of the genetic disorders that affected the parent breeds and also has a hypoallergenic coat. These are a unique breed not only in terms of their fluffy appearance but also in their calm and confident temperament. These dog breed have huge personalities wrapped up in a small cuddly package! But what is it that makes these dogs so popular?

Introduction

There is no short answer to this question because, with Yorkie Poos, there is just so much to love.

The Yorkie Poo is more than just a pet; it is a loyal, protective and loving companion. These dogs are trainable, cuddly and energetic, plus they are very great family pets and relates well with children. If you are thinking about adopting a dog or purchasing a puppy, the Yorkie Poo is definitely a great breed to consider. Before you bring a Yorkie Poo home, however, you should be a responsible dog owner and learn everything you can about this breed and how to care for it properly.

Fortunately, this ultimate guide will teach you on how to be the best Yorkie Poo dog owner you can be! Inside this book, you will find tons of helpful information about Yorkie Poo dog; how they live, how to deal with them and realize the great benefits of owning one!

This book includes information about creating the ideal habitat and diet for your dog as well as tips for breeding and showing your Yorkie Poo. You will also find in-depth health information for the breed including common health problems affecting it and the treatment options available.

The great world of Yorkie Poo breed awaits! What are you waiting for? Keep reading!

Glossary of Dog Terms

AKC – American Kennel Club, the largest purebred dog registry in the United States

Almond Eye – Referring to an elongated eye shape rather than a rounded shape

Apple Head – A round-shaped skull

Balance – A show term referring to all of the parts of the dog, both moving and standing, which produce a harmonious image

Beard – Long, thick hair on the dog's underjaw

Best in Show – An award given to the only undefeated dog left standing at the end of judging

Bitch – A female dog

Bite – The position of the upper and lower teeth when the dog's jaws are closed; positions include level, undershot, scissors, or overshot

Blaze – A white stripe running down the center of the face between the eyes

Board – To house, feed, and care for a dog for a fee

Breed – A domestic race of dogs having a common gene pool and characterized appearance/function

Breed Standard – A published document describing the look, movement, and behavior of the perfect specimen of a particular breed

Buff – An off-white to gold coloring

Clip – A method of trimming the coat in some breeds

Coat – The hair covering of a dog; some breeds have two coats, and outer coat and undercoat; also known as a double coat. Examples of breeds with double coats include German Shepherd, Siberian Husky, Akita, etc.

Condition – The health of the dog as shown by its skin, coat, behavior, and general appearance

Crate – A container used to house and transport dogs; also called a cage or kennel

Crossbreed (Hybrid) – A dog having a sire and dam of two different breeds; cannot be registered with the AKC

Dam (bitch) – The female parent of a dog;

Dock – To shorten the tail of a dog by surgically removing the end part of the tail.

Double Coat – Having an outer weather-resistant coat and a soft, waterproof coat for warmth; see above.

Drop Ear – An ear in which the tip of the ear folds over and hangs down; not prick or erect

Entropion – A genetic disorder resulting in the upper or lower eyelid turning in

Fancier – A person who is especially interested in a particular breed or dog sport

Fawn – A red-yellow hue of brown

Feathering – A long fringe of hair on the ears, tail, legs, or body of a dog

Groom – To brush, trim, comb or otherwise make a dog's coat neat in appearance

Heel – To command a dog to stay close by its owner's side

Hip Dysplasia – A condition characterized by the abnormal formation of the hip joint

Inbreeding – The breeding of two closely related dogs of one breed

Kennel – A building or enclosure where dogs are kept

Litter – A group of puppies born at one time

Markings – A contrasting color or pattern on a dog's coat

Mask – Dark shading on the dog's foreface

Mate – To breed a dog and a bitch

Neuter – To castrate a male dog or spay a female dog

Pads – The tough, shock-absorbent skin on the bottom of a dog's foot

Parti-Color – A coloration of a dog's coat consisting of two or more definite, well-broken colors; one of the colors must be white

Pedigree – The written record of a dog's genealogy going back three generations or more

Pied – A coloration on a dog consisting of patches of white and another color

Prick Ear – Ear that is carried erect, usually pointed at the tip of the ear

Puppy – A dog under 12 months of age

Purebred – A dog whose sire and dam belong to the same breed and who are of unmixed descent

Saddle – Colored markings in the shape of a saddle over the back; colors may vary

Shedding – The natural process whereby old hair falls off the dog's body as it is replaced by new hair growth.

Sire – The male parent of a dog

Smooth Coat – Short hair that is close-lying

Spay – The surgery to remove a female dog's ovaries, rendering her incapable of breeding

Trim – To groom a dog's coat by plucking or clipping

Undercoat – The soft, short coat typically concealed by a longer outer coat

Wean – The process through which puppies transition from subsisting on their mother's milk to eating solid food

Whelping – The act of birthing a litter of puppies

Chapter One: Yorkie Poo in Focus

Yorkie Poos may often time look like your cute crush, your proud parent, your loyal friend, your playful sibling or that very adorable kid you always wanted. In whatever attitude or mood it appeals, you can expect it to be confident, lively, smart, adorable, and a caring devoted pet you've always dreamed of.

The Yorkie Poo is a designer breed of dog that is irresistibly cute and sassy but it may not be the right choice for everyone. Before you decide whether or not it might be the right pet for you and your family, you need to learn and invest a significant amount of time in getting to know these animals.

In this chapter you will receive an introduction to the Yorkie Poo breed including some basic facts and information as well as the history of how it came about. This information, in combination with the practical information about keeping Yorkie Poo dogs in the next chapter, will help you decide if this is the perfect dog companion for you.

Facts About Yorkie Poos

Yorkie Poos are small-sized adaptable dogs that loves to perform tricks, cheer people up and have a knack for a good time but don't let their cuteness fool you, these dogs are also known for being a protective house pet and will confidently barked at you if they feel that their owners are being threatened. These dogs make great watchdogs and also a clown in disguise. What a great combination!

These dogs have small fluffy heads and they usually have black, medium- sized, round-shaped eyes that are not bulging with small-sized, triangular ears that maybe erect and also have a short silky coat. The most common colors for the Yorkie Poo breed include cream, black, white, red, sable, apricot, tan, chocolate, gray, and silver with mix markings.

As gorgeous as they may appear, unfortunately these dogs are not qualified for dog a show because it is not yet recognized by the American Kennel Club (AKC) and is classified as a designer breed.

The Yorkie Poo is a breed that was originally developed as a small-sized low maintenance dog with hypoallergenic coat that is perfectly suited for families and for sensitive people and that is also free of the genetic disorders that affected the parent breeds. Yorkie Poos are built to be a house companion and also serve as a watchdog. The Yorkie Poo is a very active, agile, intelligent dog and a highly trainable breed, this hybrid dog also have wide variety of sizes and weight created by breeders and dog enthusiasts. Yorkie Poos are very loyal and only trust people with whom they form very strong bonds with; they may tend to greet intruders with glee and excitement because they are naturally people-oriented but they know how to deal with it.

Yorkie Poos often described as a "clown in disguise" are confident by nature, though they can be a little bit witty around strangers. Proper socialization and training from a young age will help prevent the Yorkie Poo from being suspicious of new people. Yorkie Poos do very well as family pets and they can also be good with children.

This breed needs and loves a firm and consistent training; they are bold and they're great protectors to their owners, very ideal as first pets. Yorkie Poos, like other dogs, have a tendency to have unstable, aggressive temperaments which can be also dangerous to innocent strangers, that's why socialization and training at an early age is highly recommended.

The Yorkie Poo stands about 7 to 10 inches tall at maturity and there is only a slight difference in size between males and females of the breed. These dogs weigh between 5 and 12 pounds on average. Since the Yorkie Poo is a very active and agile dog, it has a great deal of energy and needs a lot of daily exercise to work off that energy. The Yorkie Poo doesn't require regular or excessive amount of exercise and it can adapt to almost any kind of environment, they are generally curious yet controllable indoors as long as they get enough mental and physical stimulation during the day and has proper house training.

The average lifespan for the Yorkie Poo is between 12 and 15 years and the breed is very healthy in general. Like many small dogs, however, the Yorkie Poo is prone to health issues such as cataracts, retinal detachment, dry eye, corneal dystrophy, keratitis, hypoglycemia, and progressive retinal atrophy which will be tackled in the next few chapters later on in this book. In terms of grooming, the Yorkie Poo is considered a low-shredder. These dogs don't shed too much but in order to keep their coat and skin healthy, a daily brushing is required.

Quick Facts

Pedigree: Hybrid of Yorkshire Terrier and Miniature/Toy Poodle

Group: Not Applicable; Not recognized in American Kennel Club (AKC)

Breed Size: Small

Height: 7 – 10 inches (18 – 25 cm)

Weight: 5 to 12 pounds

Coat Length: straight, curly short coat

Coat Texture: fine, silky, smooth

Color: cream, black, white, red, sable, apricot, tan, chocolate, gray, and silver

Markings: mix markings

Ears: erect; small, triangular in shape

Temperament: loyal, confident, obedient, agile, active, social

Strangers: may be wary around strangers

Other Dogs: generally good with other dogs if properly trained and socialized

Other Pets: friendly with other pets but if not properly introduce may result to potential aggression

Training: agile, intelligent and very trainable

Exercise Needs: very active; doesn't require regular or excessive amount of exercise

Health Conditions: generally healthy but predisposed to cataracts, retinal detachment, dry eye, corneal dystrophy, keratitis, hypoglycemia, and progressive retinal atrophy

Lifespan: average 12 to 15 years

Yorkie Poo Breed History

Yorkie Poo is a relatively young cross breed of dog; these dogs are a mixture of a Toy or Miniature Poodle and a Yorkshire Terrier. Yorkie Poos have been around for about a decade already and its popularity is continuously growing; these new hybrid was originally developed in an attempt to create a small low maintenance toy – sized dog that is free from genetic disorders of their parent breed and also possess a hypoallergenic coat that produces little dander, perfectly suited for allergic dog owners.

The success of crossing the Poodle with the Yorkshire Terrier has had mixed results, but some breeders have concentrated on multigenerational crosses in an effort to see the Yorkie Poo produce offspring who is more consistent to the desired traits. Most Yorkie Poo litters are still the result of first-generation breeding and it is classified as a designer breed.

Unfortunately, the breed is not yet recognized by the American Kennel Club (AKC), however it is still recognized by several breed clubs both in U.S. and internationally. These clubs are American Canine Hybrid Club (ACHC), Designer Dogs Kennel Club (DDKC), Dog Registry of America, Inc. (DRA), Designer Breed Registry (DBR), and International Designer Canine Registry (IDCR).

Today, more dog enthusiasts and pet lovers wanted Yorkie Poos because not only are they low maintenance and generally easy to care for, they are also an affectionate and devoted companion. However, there are no official registries or breed groups for Yorkie Poos, but efforts have begun to create these kinds of groups for breeders.

Chapter Two: Yorkie Poo Requirements

Are you now thinking of getting a Yorkie Poo dog? Awesome! After knowing what they are, their behaviors, and how to deal with them, it's time to give you practical tips on what you need to know before buying one.

In this chapter, you will get a whole lot of information on its pros and cons, its average associated costs as well as the licensing you need so that you will be well on your way to becoming a legitimate Yorkie Poo pet owner – should you decide to be one! It's up to you! Read on!

License Requirements

If you are planning to acquire a Yorkie Poo as your pet, there are certain restrictions and regulations that you need to be aware of. Licensing requirements for pets varies in different countries, regions, and states.

In the United States there are no federal requirements for licensing dogs or even cats – these rules are regulated at the state level. While it is true that most states do not have a mandatory requirement for people to license their dogs, it is always a good idea to do so because it will not only serve as protection for your pet but also for you.

Here are some things you need to know regarding the acquirement of Yorkie Poo dogs both in United States and in Great Britain.

United States Licensing for Dogs

As mentioned earlier, there are no federal requirements for licensing dogs in the United States they are only determined at the state level. Licensing requirements vary from one state to another, but most states do require dog owners to register and license their dogs.

In order to obtain a license for your dog you will have to provide proof that your dog has been vaccinated against rabies.

Once you obtain the license you will then have to renew it each year along with your dog's rabies vaccination. Dog licenses only cost about $25 (£16.25) per year, which is not a big expense. There might be additional requirements that need to be submitted in other states. The license will be considered temporary status until all documents are received.

Even if your state or region does not require you to license your dog, it is still a good idea to do so. If your dog escapes or gets lost, having him properly identified will significantly increase the chances of you finding him. A dog license is attached to an identification number which is linked to you – if someone finds your dog; they will be able to find your contact information through the license. You can also add an ID tag to your dog's collar along with his license for good measure.

Great Britain Licensing for Dogs

In Great Britain, licensing requirements for pets are a little different than they are in the United States. In Great Britain, it is mandatory for dog owners to license their dogs. The main difference, however, is that British dog owners do not need to vaccinate their dogs against rabies because the disease has been eradicated. Dog licenses are renewed annually and they are not a significant expense.

In some cases you will need to get a special permit if you plan to travel with your dog into or out of the country.

How Many Yorkie Poo Should You Keep?

There are several important factors you need to consider when answering this question. The question is do you have the space and the financial ability to provide for more than one dog? Yorkie Poos are a small, and generally a low maintenance breed but they still require a good deal of time and attention – think carefully before buying more than one of them. If you do have the time and money to care for another dog, your Yorkie Poo might appreciate having another dog of its kind around to keep him company while you are away.

Ideally one or two Yorkie Poo dogs are fine; just make sure that before you get another one, you can provide for the needs of both dogs. As long as you socialize your Yorkie Poo from a young age, they shouldn't have trouble getting along with each other or with other dogs.

Do Yorkie Poos Get Along with Other Pets?

For the most part, Yorkie Poos get along with other pets as long as they have been properly socialized from a young age, however these dogs small as they are, are not aware of their own size that's why they tend to launch themselves towards larger dogs. In order to prevent potentially disastrous consequences, introduce your dog to larger dogs under supervision, before they interact on their own. It is also important to note that huge dogs shouldn't be around smaller ones because they seem them as prey.

If you are going to have other household pets around such as cats, it is wise to properly introduce them and also monitor their interaction to make sure they're getting along. Be more cautious when introducing strangers, even if dogs are man's best friend, they still might be sensitive to new faces, so do it properly.

Ease and Cost of Care

Owning a Yorkie Poo doesn't come cheap! The fact that these dogs are high maintenance requires a need to provide supplies and be able to cover the expenses in order to maintain a healthy lifestyle and environment for your pet.

These things will definitely add up to your daily budget, and the cost will vary depending on where you buy it; the brand of the accessories, the nutrients included in its food and the time being. If you want to seriously own a Yorkie Poo as a pet you should be able to cover the necessary costs it entails.

In this section you will receive an overview of the expenses associated with purchasing and keeping a Yorkie Poo dog such as food and treats, grooming and cleaning supplies, toys, veterinary care, and other costs so that you can determine whether you are able to provide for such a dog or not.

Initial Costs

The initial expenses associated with keeping Yorkie Poo as pets include the cost of the dog itself as well as the its crate, accessories, toys, initial vaccinations, micro- chipping or licensing, spay/neuter surgery and also grooming supplies. You will find an overview of these costs below as well as the estimated total expense for keeping Yorkie Poos:

Purchase Price: average price of $765 (£623.82)

The cost to purchase a Yorkie Poo will vary depending on the breed you choose and where you get it. It is always best to purchase from a reputable breeder because it will reduce the risk for your dog developing an inherited disease. Keep in mind that the cost highly depends on the quality of the breed. If you choose to adopt, expect additional adoption fees as well. There could also be additional charges if your pet will be shipped, it can add up to the price of your puppy to some extent.

Crate: average $30 (£19.50)

Having a crate for your Yorkie Poo puppy is very important. Not only will it be used during housetraining, but it will also give your dog a space of his own where he can relax if he wants to. You'll need to purchase a fairly small crate for your Yorkie Poo puppy and you might need to buy a larger one once he reaches full size.

Food/Water Bowls: total cost of $20 (£18)

In addition of providing your Yorkie Poo dogs with a crate to sleep in, you should also make sure it has a set of high-quality food and water bowls. The best materials for these is stainless steel because it is easy to clean, cannot be easily chewed or eaten and won't acquire bacteria, another good option is ceramic.

Toys: total cost of $50 (£32.50)

Like other pets, Yorkie Poos need plenty of stimulation to keep their intelligent and curious minds entertained. Keep dog boredom at bay with fun toys for your dogs.

To start out, plan to buy an assortment of toys for your cat until you learn what kind it prefers. Total cost of toys may reach approximately $50 or more, again costs may vary depending on the brand. If your dog likes to destroy toys, you may need to set aside an additional amount of money to buy more toys.

Microchipping: $30 (£19.50)

In the United States and United Kingdom there are no federal or state requirements saying that you have to have your dog micro-chipped, but it is very ideal, as mentioned earlier, your Yorkie Poo could slip outside through an open door or window without you noticing it. If someone finds it without identification, they can take it to a shelter to have its microchip scanned.

A microchip is something that is implanted under your dog's skin and it carries a number that is linked to your contact information. The procedure takes just a few minutes to perform and it only costs about $30 on average, but in some states cost may vary and there are certain documents that you may need to submit in your local government.

Initial Vaccinations: $50 (£32.50) or more

During the first year of life, your Yorkie Poo puppy will need a variety of different vaccinations. If you purchase your puppy from a reputable breeder, he will probably already have had a few of these. Over the first few weeks after you bring your puppy home, however, he will need more. You should budget a substantial amount for initial vaccinations just to be prepared. Also if your dog has the appropriate boosters it needs, at a young age, it can definitely lengthen their life expectancy.

Spay/Neuter Surgery: $50 - $200 (£32.50 - £130)

If you don't plan to breed your Yorkie Poos you should have it neutered (for males) or spayed (for females) before 6 months of age. In females, this procedure includes surgically removing the ovaries and usually the uterus while in males, the testicles are surgically removed.

Spaying or neutering your pet decreases the likelihood of certain types of cancers and eliminates the possibility of your pet producing an unwanted offspring. The cost for this surgery will vary depending where you go and on the gender of your dog. If you go to a traditional veterinary surgeon, the cost for spay/neuter surgery could be very high but you can save money by going to a veterinary clinic. The average cost for neuter surgery is $50 to $100 and spay surgery costs about $100 to $200.

Supplies/Accessories: average $35 (££32.50)

There will be times that you may need to let your Yorkie Poo to play outside the house or even present it for a show. You might also need several dog accessories like a leash (if you're planning to train them or walk them outside) and other things like grooming materials during shows or simply repairing dog supplies. On average, extra accessories may cause at least $35 depending on brand and quality of the product.

An overview of these costs is provided for you in on the next section. Costs may vary depending on brand as well as location and the current exchange rate.

Needs	Costs
Purchase Price	$765 (£623.82)
Crate	$30 (£19.50)
Food/Water Bowl	$20 (£18)
Toys	$50 (£32.50)
Microchipping	$30 (£19.50)
Vaccinations	$50 (£32.50)
Spay/Neuter	$50 to $200 (£32.50 - £130)
Accessories	$35 (£32.50)
Total	$1,030 to $1,230 (£844.92 – £1008.98)

Monthly Costs

The monthly costs associated with keeping a Yorkie Poo can also be quite expensive. Some of the things that need to be bought on a monthly basis are food and treats, annual license renewal, toy replacements, and veterinary exams. Provided in this section is an overview of each of these costs as well as an estimate for each cost.

Food and Treats: total of $50 (£32.50)

Feeding your Yorkie Poo a healthy diet is very important for its health and wellness, especially for a very active and huge pet. A high-quality diet for dogs may not be cheap and highly depends on the brand. The right amount of nutrients should be provided to maintain its healthy and appealing physique. You should be prepared to spend around $40 for a high-quality dog food which will last you about a month. You should also include a monthly budget of at least $10 for treats.

Grooming Costs: approximately $9 to $12.50 (£8 - £11.25)

You should plan to have your Yorkie Poo professionally groomed about twice a year in order to keep his skin and coat in good health. You should budget about $10.50 (£8 - £11.25) per month.

License Renewal: average of $2.00 (£1.30)

The cost to license your Yorkie Poo is generally about $20 and you can renew the license for the same price each year, some states may cost more. License renewal cost divided over 12 months is about $2 per month.

Veterinary Exams: approximately $7.00 (£4.55)

In order to keep your Yorkie Poo healthy you should take him to the veterinarian at least twice a year; keep in mind that you may need to take him more often while he is a puppy to give him the vaccines he needs. The average cost for a vet visit is about $40 (£26) so, if you have two visits per year, it averages to about $7 (£4.55) per month.

Additional Costs: $15 (£9.75)

In addition to the cost for food, grooming, license renewal, and vet visits you will have to cover other costs on occasion. These costs may include replacements for toys, a larger collar as your puppy grows, cleaning products, and more. You won't have to cover these costs every month but you should include it in your budget to be safe.

An overview of these costs is provided for you in on the next section. Costs may vary depending on brand as well as location and the current exchange rate.

Needs	Monthly Costs
Food and Treats	$50 (£32.50)
Grooming Costs	$9 to $12.50 (£8 - £11.25)
License Renewal	$2 (£1.30)
Veterinary Exams	$7 (£4.55)
Other Costs	$15 (£9.75)
Total	$83 to $95.50 (£68.09 – £78.34)

Pros and Cons of Yorkie Poo

Before you bring a Yorkie Poo home you should take the time to learn the pros and cons of the breed. Every dog breed is different so you need to think about the details to determine whether the Yorkie Poo is actually the right pet for you.

In this section you will find a list of pros and cons for the Yorkie Poo dog breed:

Pros for the Yorkie Poo Breed

- A small and cute dog breed that is perfect for apartments and even houses with no yards

- Confident and bold yet generally people - oriented even with strangers
- It has hypoallergenic coat that is suited for allergic or sensitive owners
- Doesn't require extensive exercises
- Compared to other hybrids, Yorkie Poo is more intelligent, agile and very responsive to training
- Coat is fairly easy to care for with regular brushing and combing, they are a non to low – shredder breed
- Makes a good watch dog
- Generally good other family pets
- Very loyal and funny, forms strong bonds with family
- Friendly and easy-going breed in most cases, can be ideal as first pet
- A truly great companion

Cons for the Yorkie Poo Breed

- A small dog who loves to bark constantly and consistently; proper training is needed
- Not recommended for homes with very young children
- Can destroy house furniture when bored or left alone too much
- Can suffer from separation anxiety when left for a long period of time

- Can be aggressive and wary towards people when not raised or properly trained
- Has a tendency to launch themselves at larger dogs which can cause injuries
- A dog who is sometimes stubborn and witty
- Can be prone to sickness inherited from its parent breed.

Chapter Three: Tips in Buying a Yorkie Poo

Now that you are already aware and have prior knowledge about the legal aspects of owning and maintaining a Yorkie Poo as well as its pros and cons, the next step is purchasing one through a local pet store or a legitimate breeder.

In this chapter you will find valuable information about where to find a Yorkie Poo breeder, how to select a reputable breeder, and how to choose a healthy puppy from a litter. You will also receive tips for puppy-proofing your home and for introducing your new Yorkie Poo puppy to your family.

Finding a Reputable Yorkie Poo Breeder

Once you've decided that the Yorkie Poo is the right dog for you, your next step is to find one. Purchasing a Yorkie Poo might be as easy as stopping in to your local pet store since it is such a popular breed, but you should ask yourself whether this is really the best option. Many pet stores receive their puppies from puppy mills – organizations which breed dogs as quickly as they can, keeping the dogs in squalid conditions. As a result of irresponsible breeding practices, the puppies are often malnourished or suffering from health problems. The best way to make sure you get a Yorkie Poo puppy in good health is to do your research and to purchase one from a reputable Yorkie Poo breeder.

Tips in Choosing a Reputable Breeder

The difference between a reputable breeder and a puppy producer is that the former spends large amounts of time and money on the best interest of the breed, while the latter is often motivated by profit. However, in order to find a good Yorkie Poo breeder, you may have to do some research first. Once you've compiled a list of several Yorkie Poo breeders you then need to go through them to choose the best option. You don't want to run the risk of purchasing a puppy from a hobby breeder or from someone who doesn't follow responsible breeding practices. Keep in mind that when you purchase a Yorkie Poo puppy you are making a 12 to 15-year commitment!

Here are the following things you need to do to help you find a reputable Yorkie Poo breeder:

- Ask around at veterinary offices, groomers, and pet stores for referrals to Yorkie Poo breeders and assemble as much information as you can about each one.

- Visit the website for each breeder (if they have one) and check to see if the breeder is registered with a national or local breed club

- Contact each breeder individually and ask them questions about their knowledge of the Yorkie Poo breed as well as their breeding experience.

- Ask specific questions about the breeder's program and the dogs used to produce the puppies. Ask what the breeder does to prevent the passing of congenital conditions to the puppies.

- Remove the breeders from your list who do not seem to be knowledgeable about the breed or if they seem to be just hobby breeders looking to make a buck.

- Eliminate breeders from your list who refuse to answer your questions or who do not seem genuinely concerned for the wellbeing of their puppies.

- Schedule a visit with several breeders and ask for a tour of the facilities – check to make sure they are clean and that the dogs look healthy.

- Narrow down your list of breeders and make your selection – you should also ask about the breeder's preferences for putting down a deposit on a puppy.

- Place your deposit to reserve a puppy – in the next section you will receive tips for choosing a puppy from a litter.

Rescue Dogs Adoption

As an alternative to purchasing a Yorkie Poo puppy from a legitimate breeder, you should also consider adopting a rescue dog. Not only will you be doing your part in the war against puppy mills, but you will be providing a homeless dog with a loving home and new lease on life. There are many benefits associated with adopting a rescue dog and you might even be able to find a purebred Yorkie Poo or a Yorkie Poo puppy.

Adoption is much more affordable than purchasing a purebred puppy from a breeder and the dog is likely to have already been housebroken and may also have some amount of obedience training as well.

List of Breeders and Rescue Websites

In this section, you'll be given recommended websites on reputable breeders as well as rescue dogs associations in United States and United Kingdom, once you have narrow down your list of breeders, you can go and check to see the best option for you.

U.S. Yorkie Poo Breeders

Green Field Puppies
<https://www.greenfieldpuppies.com/yorkiepoo-puppies-for-sale-pa-md-de/>

Sunday Puppies
<http://sunnydaypuppies.com/>

Breeders Club
<http://www.breedersclub.net/html/breeds/yorkiepoo.php>

Norcal Pups
<http://norcalpups.com/yorkie-poo-puppies-for-sale>

Lakel and Kennel
<http://www.lakelandkennel.com/yorkiepoopuppiescurrent.htm>

Windsor Oak Farm
<http://www.windsoroakfarm.com/>

Lancaster Puppies
<https://www.lancasterpuppies.com/puppy-search/breed/yorkiepoo>

Amanda's Yorkie Poos
<http://amandaspoos.com/>

Healthy Pups
<http://www.healthypups.com/yorkiepoo>

Local Puppy Breeders
<http://www.localpuppybreeders.com/yorkie-poo-puppies-for-sale-in-north-carolina/>

Premier Pups
<https://premierpups.com/yorkie-poo-puppies-for-sale>

U.S. Yorkie Poo Recues

Yorkie and Small Dog Rescue
<http://yasdr.org/>

Poo-Mix Rescue
<http://poomixrescue.com/>

Florida Yorkie Rescue
<http://www.floridayorkierescue.com/>

Yorkie 911 Rescue
<http://www.yorkie911rescue.com/>

Save a Yorkie Rescue
<http://www.saveayorkierescue.org/>

Yorkie Haven Rescue
<http://www.yorkiehavenrescue.com/adoptable.php>

Adopt-a-Pet
<http://www.adoptapet.com/s/adopt-a-yorkie?>

U.K. Yorkie Poo Breeders

WentWood Puppies
<http://www.wentwoodpuppies.co.uk/content/yorkiepoos-
yorkiechons>

Local Puppy Breeders UK

<http://www.localpuppybreeders.co.uk/yorkie-poo-puppies-for-sale-in-the-uk/>

Pexswillow Dogs UK
<http://www.pexswillowdogs.co.uk/small-crossbreeds>

Kelly's Kennels
<http://www.kellyskennels.co.uk/>

U.K. Yorkie Poo Rescues

Little Dog Rescue UK
<http://www.littledogrescue.co.uk/index.html>

Many Tears Rescue UK
<http://www.manytearsrescue.org/>

Selecting a Healthy Yorkie Poo

Yorkie Poos on average can live for up to 12 years and more!! These breed are long time companions, and its longevity highly depends on how your chosen breeders took care of them especially when they were young. This section will give you simple tips on how you can spot a healthy Yorkie Poo puppy that you can keep for life!

- **Behavior:** Puppies should be active and playful, and loves to interact with people or with other pets. Play with the puppies to get a feel for their individual temperaments then pick the one that suits you best.

- **Ability:** Find a puppy that can run or walk normally, and does not have any mobility issues.

- **Dealing with Humans:** Pick up a puppy and hold him to see how he responds to human contact. Look for signs that the puppies are nervous or fearful of people; they shouldn't run away or hide when you approach them.

- **Puppy Interaction:** Step back and observe the puppies as a litter. Watch how they interact with each other and make sure they display normal puppy behavior.

- **Appetite:** If possible, watch the puppies being fed to make sure they have a healthy appetite and no problems eating solid food.

- **Body Appearance:** Examine the puppies' body for signs of any illness and potential injury. There should be no swelling or discoloration on the body.

- **Coat:** The texture of the puppy's coat should be smooth and has a fine texture. Look for any signs of fleas or any other pests within its coat.

- **Eyes:** The eyes should be clear and bright with no discharge.

- **Ears:** The ears should be clean and clear with no discharge such as wax or filmy material or signs of inflammation.

- **Mouth and Teeth:** Look out for any excessive drooling or unusual discharge.

- **Belly or Stomach:** Look out for a distended or swollen tummy area. Also make sure there are no lumps or unusual curves around the belly.

- **Anal Area:** The anal area should be clean. Try lifting the puppy's tail gently and look for any signs of diarrhea.

Important Note

A reputable breeder won't let you take home a puppy that is younger than 8 weeks. Some states even have laws which prohibit the sale of puppies less than 8 weeks of age.

It is important to wait until the puppy is fully weaned and eating solid food before you bring him home.

Tips on How to Puppy-Proof Your Home

Yorkie Poos, like any other dogs are curious by nature, so it's important to dog-proof your house before bringing home your new pet, not only for its safety but also yours. Here are some tips on how to prepare your home for your new found pet:

- Place all of your food in tightly lidded containers and store them in the cupboard or pantry.

- Make sure your trashcan has a tight-fitting lid and store your garbage out of your puppy's reach.

- Pick up small objects from the floor and put them away – this includes things like toys, rubber bands, pieces of string, etc.

- Store all of your medications (prescription and over-the-counter) safely in a medicine cabinet.

- Keep all of your cleaning supplies stored away where your puppy can't get into them – this includes supplies kept in the garage.

- Remove any toxic houseplants from your home or move your plants so they are well out of your puppy's reach.

- Check to make sure none of the plants on your property are toxic to dogs – if they are, remove them or fence them off so your puppy can't get into them.

- Cover any open bodies of water that could pose a drowning hazard for your puppy – this includes toilets, sinks, ponds, pools, and more.

- Make sure all of the outlets in your home are protected by plastic covers.

- Tie up the cords for your blinds as well as electric cords so your puppy can't chew on them.

These are just a few of the many things you should do to keep your puppy safe at home and keep your home intact! After going through the items on this list, walk around your house and view things from your puppy's eyes – remove anything that he might be tempted to chew on or play with that could be harmful.

Chapter Four: Caring Guidelines for Yorkie Poos

The Yorkie Poo makes a wonderful pet largely due to his sassy yet affectionate personality, but these dogs are also very adaptable to different types of living situations. In this chapter you will find some basic information about cultivating a happy and healthy home life for your Yorkie Poo. You will find tips for setting up your Yorkie Poo's crate as well as valuable information about making sure your Yorkie Poo's exercise needs are met.

Ideal Habitat Requirements for Yorkie Poos

The great thing about Yorkie Poos is that they don't take up too much space to roam around with, but aside from space, the main thing your Yorkie Poo needs in terms of its habitat is lots of love and affection from his human companions and adequate daily exercise. Even though the Yorkie Poo is sometimes stubborn and bold, it is a very loyal and loving breed that bonds closely with family, so you should make an effort to spend some quality time with your Yorkie Poo each and every day. If your Yorkie Poo doesn't get enough attention he may be more likely to develop problem behaviors like chewing or excessive barking and potential aggression as well as separation anxiety.

In addition to playing with your Yorkie Poo and spending time with him every day, you also need to make sure that his needs for exercise are met. The Yorkie Poo doesn't require extensive exercises but it is still recommended to take your dog for a walk or run once in a while plus some active play time, this is very important for your Yorkie Poo. You should also make sure your Yorkie Poo gets plenty of mental stimulation from interactive toys and games.

Supplies and Equipment for Your Yorkie Poo

In order to care for your Yorkie Poo properly you will need to have certain supplies on hand. Most importantly, your Yorkie Poo needs a crate or carrier to sleep in (you will also use it for housetraining) as well as food and water dishes and other accessories.

Below is the list of required supplies and accessories for your dog:

- Crate or carrier
- Blanket or dog bed
- Food and water dishes
- Toys (assortment)
- Collar, leash and harness
- Grooming supplies

Crate or Carrier

Having a crate or carrier for your Yorkie Poo serves two important functions. First, it will give your Yorkie Poo a place to sleep as well as a place to retire to if he needs some time to himself. Second, it will play an important role in housebreaking your Yorkie Poo. Choose a carrier that is just large enough for your Yorkie Poo to comfortably stand up, turn around, sit, and lie down in. You may need to purchase one crate for your Yorkie Poo as a puppy and upgrade it once he reaches full size.

Blanket or Dog Bed

To make your Yorkie Poo's crate more comfortable you will need to line it with a soft blanket or pet bed. Choose something that is comfortable but also easy to wash. While your Yorkie Poo is being housebroken, you might even want to get something waterproof.

Food/Water Dishes

Food and water dishes for dogs come in all shapes and sizes but you should choose a set that suits your dog's needs. Yorkie Poos are a large-breed dog, so don't choose anything relatively small. As mentioned in the previous chapters, stainless steel and ceramic bowls do not harbor bacteria like plastic can and they are easy to clean.

Toys

In order to keep your Yorkie Poo occupied you will need to provide him with an assortment of toys. Making sure your Yorkie Poo has plenty of toys will keep him from chewing on your furniture and it will give you something to use in playing with him.

Collar, Leash and Harness

Having a collar for your Yorkie Poo is incredibly important because you will need to attach your dog's license and ID tag to it. Choose a collar appropriate for your Yorkie Poo's size – it should fit well without being too tight or too loose. Choose a leash that won't weigh your Yorkie Poo down during walks and consider investing in a harness as well. Harnesses offer improved control over your dog's movements and they take the pressure off your dog's neck and throat.

Grooming Supplies

In order to keep your Yorkie Poo's skin and coat in good health you'll need to brush and comb him several times a week. Have a soft brush on hand as well as wide-toothed comb. You may also want to buy an undercoat rake to help remove dead hairs from your Yorkie Poo's coat before he sheds them all over your furniture.

Once you have assembled all of these items you can use them to create a living space for your Yorkie Poo. You will find tips for setting up your Yorkie Poo's crate in the next section of this book.

Setting Up Your Yorkie Poo's Crate

Once you have assembled all the necessary supplies you can set up your Yorkie Poo's crate. It is a good idea to set up your dog's crate in an area that gives him some space to call his own.

Here are some tips on how to set up a crate:

- Choose a room that isn't in the center of the action, but it shouldn't be too secluded either.
- The location should offer enough space for you to set up a puppy play pen in addition to your dog's crate and supplies.
- Place the crate in the play pen or build a wall around the area surrounding the crate to create your own pen.
- Make sure you place your puppy's food and water bowls nearby as well as a box of his toys.

Chapter Five: Nutritional Needs of Yorkie Poo

Feeding your Yorkie Poo dog is not that complicated. However, its level of activity should be taken into consideration to meet its nutritional diet. They're sometimes finicky eaters so it is highly recommended that dogs, like many other pets, should be given the right amount of recommended food for a balanced nutrition because proper diet can lengthen the life expectancy of your dog.

In this section, you'll learn the majority of your pet's nutritional needs as well as feeding tips and foods that are good and harmful.

The Nutritional Needs of Dogs

Like all living things, dogs require a balance of protein, fats, and carbohydrates in their diet as well as certain vitamins and minerals. When you think about the proper diet for dogs, you probably already know that meat plays an important role. This is true, but you should not overlook the other nutrients your dog needs.

In this section you will find an overview of the nutrients essential to your dog's diet and where they come from:

Carbohydrate

Dogs do not have specific requirements for carbohydrate in their diet, but carbohydrates do provide dietary fiber as well as valuable vitamins and minerals. Your dog should get his carbohydrate from whole grains like brown rice or oatmeal – these are the most digestible sources. Gluten-free and grain-free alternatives like sweet potato and tapioca are also good choices. Just be sure to avoid low-quality carbohydrates made from corn and soy ingredients because they provide very little nutritional value – dog food companies just use them to add bulk to their products without increasing cost or nutritional value.

Fats

Fat is the most highly concentrated source of energy available to your dog. Like protein, fats should come from animal-based sources like chicken fat and fish oil instead of plant-based sources like flaxseed or canola oil. You should make sure your Yorkie Poo gets a balance of omega-3 and omega-6 fatty acids to ensure proper skin and coat health.

Protein

Protein is made up of amino acids and it is incredibly important for the growth and development of your Yorkie Poo's tissues, organs, and cells. Dogs require animal-based proteins like fresh meat and meat meals because it provides them with the essential amino acids they cannot produce on their own. Plant-based proteins are less biologically valuable for your dog, though they are not essentially harmful.

Vitamins

Your dog needs to get certain vitamins from his diet because his body cannot produce them on his own. The most important vitamins for dogs are vitamin D, vitamin A, vitamin C and vitamin E.

Minerals

Minerals are inorganic compounds, because of that your dog's body cannot synthesize them; it must come from his diet. The most important minerals for dogs include copper, calcium, phosphorus, potassium, sodium, and iron.

Water

In addition to macronutrients and micronutrients, your Yorkie Poo also needs plenty of fresh water on a daily basis. About 70% of your dog's bodyweight is made up of water so, if he doesn't drink enough water during the day, it can have a serious negative impact on his health.

How to Select a Healthy Dog Food Brand

Now that you have a basic understanding of your Yorkie Poo's nutritional needs you can think about shopping for a high-quality dog food. Your Yorkie Poo should be fed a high-quality dry kibble dog food that is specially formulated for small-breed dogs. It is highly recommended that you mixed a tiny amount of canned food into the kibble to entice your Yorkie Poos to eat. Without dry food, the Yorkie-Poo has a great potential to develop gum disease, bad breath and tooth loss.

Many dog food companies offer formulas for puppies as well as adults, so choose the formula that is right for your Yorkie Poo, depending on his age.

Shopping for dog food can be difficult because there are so many different options to choose from. In order to separate the high-quality foods from the low-quality foods, you need to learn how to read a dog food label. When comparing dog foods, the first thing you want to look for is the AAFCO statement of nutritional adequacy – this will tell you that the product meets the basic nutritional needs of dogs. AAFCO is the American Association of Feed Control Officials and the statement of nutritional adequacy will look something like this:

"[Product Name] is formulated to meet the nutritional levels established by the AAFCO Dog Food nutrient profiles for [Life Stage]."

After you've determined that the product is approved by AAFCO, you can then take a more detailed look at the ingredients list. Remember, protein is the most important nutritional consideration for dogs so you should look for a high-quality source of protein (or two) at the top of the ingredients list. Ingredients lists for dog foods are assembled in descending order by volume – this means that the ingredients at the top of the list are present in the highest quantities. So, if a product lists something like deboned chicken or fresh turkey as the first ingredient, you can assume that the product is a good source of protein.

When perusing dog food labels, you are likely to come across meat meals like chicken meal or salmon meal. The word "meal" might turn you off, but it is actually a very good ingredient to have in a dog food. Fresh meats contain up to 80% water so, by the time the product is cooked, the actual volume of the meat is much lower than it was originally. Meat meals have already been cooked down to a moisture level around 10% so they are actually a much more concentrated source of protein than fresh meat.

In addition to high-quality proteins, you should also look for digestible carbohydrates like whole grains and fresh vegetables. Things like brown rice and oatmeal are valuable additions to a commercial dog food while products like corn gluten meal or wheat flour are not. Gluten-free and grain-free carbohydrates like sweet potato and tapioca starch are also good ingredients if you are looking for a product that is free from gluten and grains. Just try to avoid byproduct meals as well as corn and soy ingredients. When it comes to fats, you should look for animal-based fats like chicken fat and salmon oil – these are much more biologically valuable to your dog than plant-based fats like canola oil or flaxseed. You should look for a blend of both omega-3 and omega-6 fatty acids as well.

Not only do you need to be mindful of the ingredients included in your dog's food, but you should also be mindful of things that are NOT included. Avoid products made with artificial preservatives like BHT and BHA. You also want to look for products free from artificial flavors, colors and dyes. If your Yorkie Poo suffers from food allergies, consider a Limited Ingredient Diet (LID) which is made with a novel source of protein that won't trigger his allergies. Novel sources of protein might include things like bison, venison, or even kangaroo meat.

Tips for Feeding Your Yorkie Poo

When it comes to feeding your Yorkie Poo, you may be wondering how much food is too much. The Yorkie Poo is one of the many breeds prone to obesity and once your dog becomes obese it can be difficult for him to lose weight. Your best bet is to follow the feeding recommendations on the dog food package as a starting place. Follow the feeding recommendations for a few weeks and keep an eye on your Yorkie Poo's weight. If he starts to gain weight, you may need to cut back on his portions a little bit. If your dog loses weight or doesn't appear to have as much energy as he used to, you may need to feed him a little bit more.

Another important thing to consider in feeding your Yorkie Poo is how many times you should feed him per day.

While your Yorkie Poo is still a puppy, you might be able to feed him freely instead of rationing his meals. Just keep in mind that your Yorkie Poo puppy will reach his maximum size more quickly, at which point you should switch him to an adult dog food formula. Monitor your Yorkie Poo puppy's growth and once he reaches about 80% of his maximum expected size, make the switch. Your veterinarian should be able to help you estimate your Yorkie Poo's maximum size.

Toxic Foods to Avoid

It might be tempting to give in to your dog when he is begging at the table, but certain "people foods" can actually be toxic for your dog. As a general rule, you should never feed your dog anything unless you are 100% sure that it is safe. In this section you will find a list of foods that can be toxic to dogs and should therefore be avoided.

- Alcohol
- Apple seeds
- Avocado
- Cherry pits

- Chocolate
- Coffee
- Garlic
- Grapes/raisins
- Hops
- Macadamia nuts
- Mold
- Mushrooms
- Mustard seeds
- Onions/leeks
- Peach pits
- Potato leaves/stems
- Rhubarb leaves
- Tomato leaves/stem
- Xylitol
- Walnuts
- Yeast Dough

If your Yorkie Poo eats any of these foods, contact the Pet Poison Control hotline right away at (888) 426 – 4435.

Chapter Six: Training Your Yorkie Poo

At some point in time, you and your pet will already get along and are comfortable in each other, strengthen your relationship by training them. Training a Yorkie Poo is not that hard to do, in fact it can be a fun and rewarding bonding experience for both of you.

There are lots of pet owners out there who have properly trained and raised a well-behaved Yorkie Poo. They are intelligent and innately design for training, that is why they can absorb information very quickly and easily as long as you do it right. Trust is the most important key in training your dog or puppy. The first thing you need to do is to be able to establish a solid connection and rapport between you and your pet.

This chapter will provide some guidelines you can do to get your dog to be well-behaved and disciplined. Are you ready? Read on!

Socializing Your Puppy

The first few weeks of your Yorkie Poo puppy's life are incredibly important. Not only is this when you will establish a bond with him, but it is also when he is the most impressionable. Socialization is essential for puppies when they are young because the experiences they have during this impressionable period will determine who they are as an adult.

If your puppy isn't properly socialized, he might turn into a shy and timid adult dog who responds to new people and unfamiliar situations with fear or uncertainty instead of normal curiosity. Fortunately, socialization for Yorkie Poo dogs is easy to grasp.

Here are some tips on how to socialize your dog so that it'll feel confident and at ease with others:

- Introduce your puppy/dog to friends in the comfort of your own home where your puppy/dog feels safe.

- Take your cdog with you to the pet store or to a friend's house so that it experiences new locations.

- Expose your puppy/dog to people of different sizes, shapes, gender, and skin color.

- Introduce your puppy/dog to children of different ages. Just supervise the kids to make sure they handle the puppy/dog safely.

- Take your puppy/dog with you in the car when you run errands, make them part of your daily routine as much as possible.

- Expose your puppy/dog to loud noises such as fireworks, cars backfiring, loud music, and thunder. It will get used to it eventually.

- Introduce your puppy/dog to various appliances and tools such as blenders, lawn mowers, vacuums, etc.

- Play with your puppy/dog using different kinds of toys and experiment with different kinds of food and treats to also see its preferences.

Tips in Training Your Yorkie Poo

In addition to socializing your new Yorkie Poo puppy you should also begin training as soon as possible. Yorkie Poos are very intelligent and eager to learn, although at times they may be witty and stubborn so starting with training early will increase your chances of having a well-behaved and obedient adult dog. When it comes to dog training, there are many different methods to choose from. Some of the most popular methods include positive reinforcement, punishment, alpha dog, and clicker training.

In the section you will find an overview of each training method below:

Positive Reinforcement

This method of training hinges on your dog's natural desire to please. In essence, you train your dog to repeat desired behaviors by rewarding him for doing them. For example, if you want your dog to sit when you give him the "Sit" command, teach him what the command means and then reward him each time he responds to the command appropriately. Positive reinforcement training is one of the most popular and effective dog training methods.

Clicker Training

This type of training is a version of positive reinforcement training and it is highly popular. The key to success with positive reinforcement training lies in helping your dog to identify the desired behavior – that is where the clicker comes in. You go through the normal process of training, giving your dog a command and guiding him to perform the desired behavior. Then, as soon as he displays the behavior you click the clicker and immediately issue a reward – this helps your dog to learn more quickly which behavior it is that you desire.

You should only use the clicker during the first few repetitions of a training sequence until your dog learns what the desired behavior is – you don't want him to become dependent on the clicker to perform that behavior.

Punishment

This type of training is almost the opposite of positive reinforcement training – rather than rewarding your dog for performing desired behaviors, you punish him for performing unwanted behaviors. The punishment used doesn't have to be violent or cruel – it can be as simple as withdrawing your attention to teach your dog to stop whining.

Give your dog the opposite of what he wants to curb the negative behavior in question. This type of training is more effective as a method for curbing negative behaviors than for teaching positive behaviors.

Alpha Dog

This type of training was made popular by the Dog Whisperer, Cesar Milan. Milan believes that dogs are natural pack animals and that dog owners must establish themselves as the leader of the dog's "pack". This means that you must make your dog submissive to you so he will submit to your will. Alpha dog training involves things like never letting the dog walk through the door before you, or waiting to feed your dog until after you have eaten. Although this training method works for some people, it is not endorsed by the ASPCA and other animal rights groups.

Tips in Housebreaking Your Yorkie Poo Puppy

After socialization, housetraining is probably one of your most important tasks as a dog owner. While your Yorkie Poo puppy is still young, he will not be physically capable of holding his bladder or bowel movements. Making sure to take your puppy outside very frequently (as often as once an hour) will help to reduce the frequency of accidents until your puppy is old enough for housetraining. The most effective method for housetraining a puppy is crate training.

Here are some useful tips for housetraining your puppy:

- Follow the guidelines provided earlier in this book to choose a crate for your puppy and set it up as directed.

- Get your puppy used to the crate by tossing treats into it and feeding him his meals in the crate.

- Eventually your puppy should be comfortable enough with the crate to take naps in it with the door open.

- Start closing the door to the crate while your puppy is inside and leave him there for a few minutes.

- Gradually increase the length of the confinement until your puppy can remain calm in the crate for at least 30 minutes.

- Start housetraining by selecting a certain area of the yard where you want your puppy to do his business.

- Take your puppy to that area each time you take him outside and give him a verbal command like "go pee".

- When your puppy does his business in the area, praise him excitedly and offer a reward to reinforce the behavior.

- Keep your puppy in the same room as you at all times when you are at home and supervise him closely.

- Take your puppy outside every hour or two, especially after naps and within 30 minutes after a meal.

- If your puppy does not do his business when you take him out, take him right back inside and try again in 30 minutes.

Important Note

When you are not at home or unable to watch your puppy, confine him to the crate – avoid leaving any food or water which might increase his risk for having an accident. Be reminded of the following:

- Be sure not to leave your puppy in the crate for longer than he is physically capable of holding his bladder and bowels.

- Gradually increase the length of the time your puppy spends in the crate until he can make it overnight.

- Always take your puppy outside immediately after releasing him from the crate and before you put him in it.

Chapter Seven: Grooming Your Yorkie Poo

Your Yorkie Poo's skin produces natural oils that help to protect its coat and keep it moisturized. Grooming for dogs is not just about keeping it clean, it is mainly about improving and maintaining the condition of the skin. Grooming your dog helps to distribute its natural body oils to keep his skin healthy, shiny, and soft. No matter what kind of coat your Yorkie Poo has, it is your job to groom it properly so it remains in good health.

In this chapter you will learn the basics about grooming your Yorkie Poo – this includes brushing and bathing your dog as well as trimming his nails, cleaning his ears, and brushing his teeth.

Recommended Tools for Grooming

The coat of Yorkie Poos varies tremendously since Yorkie Poos are a fairly new crossbreed. It may be curly, wavy or poker straight, the great part is that they don't shred a lot which means you will not need to do very much maintenance – brushing a few times a week and bathing as needed should be sufficient. Nevertheless, it is essential that you have the right tools on hand to complete the job.

Here is a list of several recommended grooming tools and supplies below:

- Soft brush
- Metal comb
- Undercoat rake
- Small, sharp scissors
- Dog-friendly shampoo
- Nail clippers
- Dog-friendly ear cleaning solution
- Dog toothbrush
- Dog-friendly toothpaste

As long as you have these supplies on hand you should be able to do most of your Yorkie Poo's grooming yourself at home. Still, you might want to have your Yorkie Poo professionally groomed twice a year for good measure.

Tips for Bathing and Grooming Yorkie Poos

Now that you know what tools and supplies you need to have on hand for grooming your Yorkie Poo you are ready to learn the process. You should brush your Yorkie Poo's coat as often as possible – at least once a day is recommended to keep your dog's skin and coat soft and silky. Another characteristic of Yorkie Poos is that they produce little dander, which is actually an advantage for allergic owners.

The first step in grooming your Yorkie Poo is to go over his body with a metal comb. Start at the back of the head and work your way down the dog's neck and back, brushing in the direction of hair growth. Move on to the dog's sides and comb the fur down each leg. Once you've gone over your Yorkie Poo with a comb to remove tangles you can do it again with the wire pin brush to collect loose and dead hairs. If for some reason your Yorkie Poo is a particularly high shedder (most Yorkie Poos blow their coats twice a year) you may also want to use an undercoat rake to remove dead hairs from the Yorkie Poo's undercoat before they can be shed.

After you've gone over your Yorkie Poo with the comb and brush he is ready for bathing. Remember, the Yorkie Poo doesn't need to be bathed frequently – you should only do it when he really needs it. If you bathe your dog too frequently it could cause his skin and coat to dry out. When you do bathe your dog, be sure to use dog-friendly shampoo that will be gentle on his skin.

Here's some guidelines for bathing your Yorkie Poo:

- Place a non-slip mat or towel on the bottom of your tub then fill it with a few inches of warm water (not hot water).

- Put your Yorkie Poo in the tub and use a handheld sprayer or a container to wet down his coat as thoroughly as possible.

- Apply a small amount of your dog-friendly shampoo to your hand then work it into your Yorkie Poo's coat, forming a thick soapy lather.

- Work the soap through the hair on your dog's neck, back, legs, chest and tail – avoid getting his ears, eyes, and nose wet.

- Thoroughly rinse away the soap using clean water until all traces have been removed.

- Use a damp washcloth to carefully clean the fur on your dog's head and face, if necessary, keeping the eyes and ears dry.

- Towel-dry your Yorkie Poo using a large fluffy towel until you have removed as much moisture from his coat as possible.

- If it is cold out and your Yorkie Poo is shivering, finish drying his coat using a hairdryer on the low heat setting.

The most important thing to remember when bathing your Yorkie Poo is that you must keep his ears dry. Wet ears are a breeding ground for bacteria and infection. The Yorkie Poo doesn't have erect ears to allow plenty of airflow to the ear canal, that's why there is a huge risk for ear infections so be very careful.

Other Grooming Tasks

In addition to brushing and bathing your Yorkie Poo, you also need to engage in some other grooming tasks including trimming your dog's nails, cleaning his ears, and brushing his teeth.

Brushing Your Yorkie Poo's Teeth

The idea of brushing your dog's teeth might sound gross but it is actually a very important part of grooming. Periodontal (dental) disease is incredibly common among pets and it can actually lead to some serious health problems including tooth loss, heart disease, and organ damage.

Here are some simple tips on how to brush your dog's teeth and mouth:

- Place a small amount of dog-friendly toothpaste on a dog toothbrush.
- Brush just a few of your dog's teeth at a time until he gets used to the process.
- Be sure to reward your dog after brushing his teeth so he learns that good behavior earns him a treat. This will make things much easier for you in the long run.

Cleaning Your Yorkie Poo's Ears

Cleaning your Yorkie Poo's ears isn't a difficult task, but he might not like it. A dog's ears are a breeding ground for bacteria so, if you do not keep them clean, your dog may have an increased risk for recurrent ear infections.

Here are some simple tips on how to brush your dog's teeth and mouth:

- Clean your dog's ears, add a few drops of a dog-safe ear cleaning solution to your dog's ear canal.
- Massage the outside of your Yorkie Poo's ears by hand to spread the solution.
- Use clean cotton balls to clean away any buildup inside your dog's ears (as well as excess cleaning solution).
- Let your dog's ears dry.

Trimming Your Yorkie Poo's Nails

When it comes to trimming your dog's nails, you need to be very careful. Each of your dog's nails contains a quick – the blood vessel that supplies blood to the nail. If you cut the nail too short and sever this blood vessel it could not only hurt your dog, but it could cause profuse bleeding as well. The best way to prevent this from happening is to make sure you have the right tool and to learn the proper nail trimming procedure before you do it yourself. Ask your vet or a professional groomer to show you how to trim your dog's nails and then, when you do it yourself, be sure to only trim away the sharp tip.

Chapter Eight: Breeding Your Yorkie Poo

If you decided to buy two dogs, for instance a male and female and keep them together, you should definitely prepare for the possibility of breeding, unless it's the same gender, otherwise you're going to be caught off guard! If you are interested in breeding your Yorkie Poo, this chapter will give you a wealth of information about the processes and phases of its breeding and you will also learn how to properly raise puppies on your own.

This not for everyone but if you want to have better understanding about how to raise these dogs, then you should definitely not miss this part! On the contrary if you are interested in becoming a reputable breeder, then this is a must read chapter for you.

Basic Dog Breeding Information

When it comes to dog breeding, no matter what breed you choose, you need to be absolutely sure of your decision before you begin. Breeding dogs of any breed is a huge responsibility and it can take a financial toll on your family as well. Unfortunately, many dog owners out there think that breeding their dogs is a good way to make some extra money. The reality is, however, that by the time you pay for healthcare costs for your pregnant female and a litter of puppies (not to mention food and housing for all of them), you will be lucky to come out even.

If you do not plan to breed your Yorkie Poo, the ASPCA recommends having him or her neutered or spayed before 6 months of age. For female dogs, they should be spayed before their first heat. Keep in mind that spaying and neutering dogs before 6 months of age can significantly reduce their risk for certain types of cancer and other serious diseases.

Mating Behavior of Dogs

The most important thing you need to learn about is the estrus cycle. This is the cycle also known as "heat" through which female dogs go about twice a year. The cycle lasts for 14 to 21 days on average and it occurs about every 6 months once it becomes regular – it can take a few years for a dog to establish a regular cycle.

Swelling of the vulva for females - dogs may also excrete a bloody discharge at the start of the cycle, though many dogs do not develop this until the 7th day of the cycle. As your Yorkie Poo's cycle progresses, the discharge will become lighter in color until it is pink and watery by the 10th day of the cycle. In addition to this discharge, many female dogs start to urinate more frequently during their cycle – they might also develop urine marking behavior to attract male dogs.

A male dog can smell a female in heat from very great distances, so you need to be very careful to keep your female Yorkie Poo indoors while she is in heat. When you take her outside, be sure to keep her on a leash and supervise her closely. Never take a female dog in heat to the dog park or to another location where intact male dogs may be present. If you intend to breed your Yorkie Poo, you want to avoid any accidental mating.

When the discharge from your dog's vulva becomes light in color and watery, this is likely when she will be the most fertile and when she will begin to ovulate – this generally happens around day 11 to 15 of the cycle. It is during this time that you want to introduce her to the male dog to make an attempt at breeding. If you introduce the dogs too early in the female's cycle she might not be receptive to him. If she isn't, just wait another day or two before trying again. Your Yorkie Poo is technically capable of conceiving at any point during her cycle because the sperm from the male dog can survive in the reproductive tract for as long as 5 days.

Tips for Breeding Your Yorkie Poo

Now that you know the basics about breeding dogs you can learn the specifics about Yorkie Poos. The Yorkie Poo has a gestation period lasting about 58 - 65 days (or about 9 weeks). The gestation period is the period of time following conception during which the puppies develop in the mother's uterus. The average litter size for the Yorkie Poo breed is between 6 to 10 puppies. Keep in mind that new mothers will often have smaller litters – the next few litters will generally be larger before the litter size starts to taper off again.

Again, the Yorkie Poo gestation period lasts about 65 days but you won't be able to tell that your Yorkie Poo is pregnant right away. By the 28th day of pregnancy or during the fourth week, it is safe to perform an ultrasound on the pregnant dog, and most likely your vet will confirm that your dog is indeed pregnant because around the 28th to 32nd day, your veterinarian will be able to feel the puppies by palpating the mother's uterus.

To increase your chances of a successful breeding, you need to keep track of your Yorkie Poo's estrus cycle. Once your female reaches the point of ovulation, you can introduce her to the male dog and let nature take its course. Breeding behavior varies slightly from one breed to another, but you can expect the male dog to mount the female from behind (as long as she is receptive). If the breeding is successful, conception will occur and the gestation period will begin.

While the puppies are developing inside your female Yorkie Poo's uterus, you need to take special care to make sure the female is properly nourished. You do not need to make changes to your dog's diet until the fourth or fifth week of pregnancy. At that point you should slightly increase her daily rations in an amount proportionate to her weight gain. It is generally best to offer your dog free feeding because she will know how much she needs to eat. Make sure your dog's diet is high in protein as well as calories and fat to support the development of her puppies – calcium is also very important.

<u>Signs that your dog is pregnant:</u>

- Fast nipple growth or appearance
- Less energetic
- More affectionate or clingy
- Experiences mood swings
- The stomach will expand and get firm
- The dog will clean herself more than the usual
- May attempt to build a nest.

Labor Process of Yorkie Poos

By the eighth week of pregnancy you should start preparing yourself and your dog for the whelping. This is the time when you should set up a whelping box where your female dog can comfortably give birth to her puppies. Place the box in a quiet, dim area and line it with newspapers and old towels for comfort. The closer it gets to the whelping, the more time your dog will spend in the whelping box, preparing it for her litter.

During the last week of your Yorkie Poo's pregnancy you should start taking her internal temperature at least once per day – this is the greatest indicator of impending labor. The normal body temperature for a dog is about 100°F to 102°F (37.7°C to 38.8°C). When your dog's body temperature drops, you can expect contractions to begin within 24 hours or so. Prior to labor, your dog's body temperature may drop as low as 98°F (36.6°C) – if it gets any lower, contact your veterinarian.

Once your Yorkie Poo starts going into labor you can expect her to show some obvious signs of discomfort. Your dog might start pacing restlessly, panting, and switching positions. The early stages of labor can often last for several hours and contractions may occur as often as 10 minutes apart. If your Yorkie Poo has contractions for more than 2 hours without any of the puppies being born, contact your veterinarian immediately. Once your dog starts giving birth, the puppies will arrive about every thirty minutes following ten to thirty minutes of straining.

After each puppy is born, the Yorkie Poo will lick the puppy clean, it may even eat the umbilical cord because it is animal instinct. This also helps to stimulate the puppy to start breathing on his own. Once all of the puppies have been born, the mother will expel the rest of the placenta (the afterbirth) and then let the puppies start nursing. It is essential that the puppies begin nursing within one hour of being born because this is when they will receive the colostrum from the mother. Colostrum is the first milk produced and it contains a variety of nutrients as well as antibodies to protect the pups until their own immune systems have time to develop. In addition to making sure that the puppies are feeding, you should also make sure that the mother eats soon after whelping.

Yorkie Poo puppies are small in size; these puppies are also born blind, with their eyes and ears closed, so they are completely dependent on the mother for several weeks. Around 3rd week, the puppies will open their eyes and their ears will become erect sometime after. As the puppies grow, they will start to become increasingly active and the will grow very quickly as long as they are properly fed by the mother.

At six weeks of age is the time you should begin weaning the puppies by offering them small amounts of puppy food soaked in water or broth. The puppies might sample small bits of solid food even while they are still nursing and the mother will general wean the puppies by week 8, with or without your help. If you plan to sell the puppies, be sure not to send them home unless they are fully weaned at least 8 weeks old. You should also take steps to start socializing the puppies from an early age to make sure they turn into well-adjusted adults.

Breeding Method used to Produce Yorkie Poos

This section provides an overview on how dog breeders produce Yorkie Poos. If you are interested in breeding on your own, you can use this as a guideline to successfully create a Yorkie Poo out of a Yorkshire Terrier and a Poodle, who knows, you might actually create a new breed!

- F1 = 50% Yorshire Terrier, 50% Poodle

    Its hair strand and coat can vary from curly to straight similar to Poodles. This mix breed will produce healthier Yorkie Poos because it is a first generation.

- F1 – B = 25% Poodle, 75% Yorkshire Terrier.

    Also known as the Yo-Yopoo with a coat similar to that of a Yorkie Poo, this breed can be achieved by breeding a Yorkiepoo with a Yorkshire Terrier.

- F1-B = 75% Poodle, 25% Yorkshire Terrier.

    A Yorkie Poo mixed with a pure bred Poodle is what you need to achieved this type.

- F2 = Yorkshire terrier paired with an F1 Yorkie Poo.

- F3 = A cross-breed of the first and second type.

Chapter Nine: Keeping Your Yorkie Poo Healthy

You as the owner should be aware of the potential threats and diseases that could harm the wellness of your Yorkie Poo. Just like human beings, you need to have knowledge on these diseases so that you can prevent it from happening in the first place. You will find tons of information on the most common problems that may affect your cat including its causes, signs and symptoms, remedies and prevention.

Common Health Problems of Yorkie Poos

In this section, you will learn about the diseases that may affect and threaten your Yorkie Poo's wellness. Learning these diseases as well as its remedies is vital for you and your dog so that you could prevent it from happening or even help with its treatment in case they caught one.

Below are some of the most common health problems that can occur to Yorkie Poo dogs. You will learn some guidelines on how these diseases can be prevented and treated as well as its signs and symptoms.

Legg-Calvé-Perthes Disease

This condition is commonly seen in miniature, toy, and small-breed dogs and it usually common during five to eight months of age. This disease involves spontaneous degeneration of the head on the femur bone, located in the dog's hind leg. This results in disintegration of the hip joint (coxofemoral) and bone and joint inflammation.

Causes

The exact cause of Legg-Calvé-Perthes Disease is unknown, but researchers suggest that dogs suffering because from this condition, have blood supply issues to the femoral head.

Signs and Symptoms

If you notice your dog showing lameness for two to three months; he is carrying its affected limbs or has pain when moving its hip joint, as well as wasting its thigh muscles on its affected limbs these are signs that your dog is suffering from this disease.

Diagnosis and Treatment

You will need to give a thorough medical history of your dog's health, including duration and frequency of symptoms. Laboratory testing is not usually required to diagnose the disease. Your vet will most likely recommend your dog for X-rays of the affected area, which should identify any changes in the femoral bone and joint. Upon further diagnosis the widening of joint space, decreased bone density, and thickening of femoral bone neck can be seen during its early stages. In advanced cases, extreme deformation of femoral head, new bone formation in the affected area, and femoral neck fracture may also be seen.

The veterinarian may also perform a complete physical examination on your dog, particularly the affected limb and hip joint area.

Patellar Luxation in Dogs

Patellar luxation is another common disease in toy and miniature dog breeds. This occurs when the dog's kneecap (patella) is dislocated from its normal anatomic position in the groove of the thigh bone (femur). Female dogs are usually the ones affected by these disease more than male dogs.

When the kneecap is dislocated from the groove of the thigh bone, it can only be returned to its normal position once the quadriceps muscles in the hind legs of the animal relax and lengthen. It is for this reason that most dogs with the condition will hold up their hind legs for a few minutes.

Causes

The main cause of Patellar Luxation or a dislocated kneecap is genetic malformation or trauma. This condition can normally be seen approximately four months after birth.

Signs and Symptoms

Usually, a dog with a dislocated kneecap will exhibit prolonged abnormal hind limb movement, occasional skipping or hind limb lameness, and sudden lameness. The specific symptoms of a dislocated kneecap will depend on the severity and persistence of the condition, as well as the amount of degenerative arthritis that is involved.

Diagnosis and Treatment

Veterinarians will usually suggest performing Craniocaudal (top view) and Mediolateral (side view) X-rays for the stifle joint, hip, and hock as well as skyline X-rays for the thigh bone. Your vet will also likely perform an examination by touch to feel for kneecap freedom.

The Craniocaudal and Mediolateral tests will detect the bending and twisting of the thigh bone and larger bone of the lower leg while Skyline X-rays may reveal a shallow, flattened, or curved groove of the thigh bone.

Aside from X-rays, a fluid sample may also be taken from the joint and an analysis of the lubricating fluid in the joint may show a small increase in mononuclear cells.

Portosystemic Shunt (PSS)

This condition is an abnormal connection between the portal vascular system and systemic circulation.

In a healthy dog, the blood that exits the intestines, spleen, and pancreas enters the portal vein, which then takes blood to the liver. The liver metabolizes and detoxifies this blood. If a shunt is present, the liver is deprived of factors that enhance liver development, these are called hepatotrophic factors; blood from the abdominal organs which should be drained by the portal vein into the liver is instead shunted to the systemic circulation by the PSS which results in failure of the liver to reach normal size (hepatic atrophy).

This means that a portion of the toxins, proteins and nutrients absorbed by the intestines bypass the liver and are shunted directly into the systemic circulation.

2 Types of Congenital Shunts
- Extrahepatic (outside the liver)
- Intrahepatic (inside the liver)

Signs and Symptoms:
Below are the common signs and symptoms of PSS, these are often episodic and are usually seen after eating. These neurological signs are due to the hepatic encephalopathy syndrome.

- ataxia (abnormal swaying)
- blindness
- head pressing
- loss of appetite or anorexia
- vomiting
- diarrhea
- seizures
- constipation
- excessive urination/drinking
- difficulty urinating
- blood in the urine or hematuria

Diagnosis

If your veterinarian confirms or suspects that your dog has PSS, he/she will advised that your dog undergo several tests and full diagnostic work-up such as blood work, urinalysis, liver function tests, radiographs, ultrasound, nuclear scintigraphy (a non-invasive technique involving colonic administration of a radioisotope), portography (X-ray dye study that specifically highlights the portal system and a CT scan.

Some of these diagnostics may be completed by your primary care veterinarian, but for its treatment and other extensive tests, you will be referred to an ACVS board-certified veterinary surgeon or veterinary specialty center.

Treatment

The only treatment for this condition is surgery; however, before undergoing surgery, your dog may need medical management to improve its health to a point where the risk of anesthesia and surgery is low. In order to medically stabilize your dog before surgery, a low protein diet and oral administration of antibiotics and lactulose will be done. The goals are to decrease the bacterial population in the intestines and to minimize the production of toxins.

Once your dog is medically stabilized, the next step is for him/her to undergo surgical attenuation (narrowing) or full ligation (tying off) of the abnormal shunt vessel for a single PSS. This full ligation may be done instantaneously using suture material or intra-venous injection of an embolus of special glue material, or delayed full ligation with an ameroid constrictor, cellophane band or an intra-venous embolic coil.

Your primary care veterinarian may refer you and your pet to an ACVS board-certified veterinary surgeon because this surgery is technically challenging and could be fatal as well.

Idiopathic Epilepsy

Epilepsy is a seizure disorder that may manifest in several different ways. In most cases, seizures are preceded by a focal onset phase during which the dog may appear dazed or frightened.

Signs and Symptoms

The dog typically falls to its side and becomes stiff, salivating profusely and paddling with all four limbs. Seizures generally last for 30 to 90 seconds and they most commonly occur while the dog is resting or asleep.

Two Types of Epilepsy:

- **Primary epilepsy** is also called true epilepsy or idiopathic epilepsy – this type of epilepsy involves seizure with an unknown cause. This condition usually presents between 6 months and 5 years of age and it may have a genetic link.

- **Secondary epilepsy** - a condition in which the cause of the seizures can be determined.

Causes and Diagnosis

As mentioned earlier, the primary epilepsy has no cause, it is most likely hereditary. The most common causes for secondary epilepsy include degenerative disease, developmental problems, toxins/poisoning, infections, metabolic disorders, nutritional deficiencies, and trauma.

Veterinarians use information about the age of onset and pattern of the seizures to make a diagnosis.

Treatments

Treatment options for canine epilepsy may involve anticonvulsant medications and monitoring of the dog's health and weight.

Hip Dysplasia

Hip dysplasia is a very common musculoskeletal problem among dogs. In a normal hip, the head of the femur (thigh bone) sits snugly within the groove of the hip joint and it rotates freely within the grove as the dog moves. Hip dysplasia occurs when the femoral head becomes separated from the hip joint – this is called subluxation. This could occur as a result of abnormal joint structure or laxity in the muscles and ligaments supporting the joint.

This condition can present in puppies as young as 5 months of age or in older dogs.

Causes and Diagnosis

Genetics are the largest risk factor for hip dysplasia, though nutrition and exercise are factors as well. Diagnosis for hip dysplasia is made through a combination of clinical signs, physical exam, and x-rays.

Signs and Symptoms

The most common symptoms of hip dysplasia include pain or discomfort, limping, hopping, or unwillingness to move. As the condition progresses, the dog's pain will increase and he may develop osteoarthritis. The dog may begin to lose muscle tone and might even become completely lame in the affected joint.

Treatments

Surgical treatments for hip dysplasia are very common and generally highly effective. Medical treatments may also be helpful to reduce osteoarthritis and to manage pain.

Degenerative Myelopathy

Degenerative myelopathy is a progressive disease which affects the spinal cord in older dogs. This disease typically manifests between 8 and 14 years of age, beginning with loss of coordination in the dog's hind limbs.

Causes and Diagnosis

This disease is caused by degeneration of the white matter in the dog's spinal cord. This degeneration may or may not be caused by the mutation of a certain gene. In order to diagnose your Yorkie Poo with degenerative myelopathy your veterinarian will perform tests to rule out other causes of the weakness. These tests may include MRI, myelography, and biopsy of the spinach cord. In many cases, however, the diagnosis cannot be completely confirmed except with an autopsy (necropsy).

Signs and Symptoms

At first the dog will wobble when walking or drag the feet – this might occur in one limb or both. As the disease progresses, the limbs become increasingly weak and the dog might have difficulty standing. Eventually, the weakness will worsen to the point of paralysis and the dog will be unable to walk.

Treatments

Unfortunately, there are no treatments available to slow or stop the progression of degenerative myelopathy. The best treatment is to manage the dog's symptoms and to keep him as comfortable as possible. The use of harnesses and carts is common for dogs that have lost the use of their hind limbs.

Glaucoma

The Yorkie Poo breed is prone to several eye-related conditions including glaucoma. Glaucoma is a very common condition in which the fluid inside the dog's eye builds and creates intraocular pressure that is too high. When the pressure inside the eye increases, it can lead to damage of the internal structures within the eye. If this condition is not treated promptly, it can lead to permanent loss of vision or total blindness for the dog.

Signs and Symptoms

Glaucoma can sometimes be difficult to diagnose in the early stages, but common signs include dilated pupil, cloudiness of the eye, and rubbing the eye. If you notice any of these symptoms, seek immediate treatment.

Treatments

Treatment options include topical solutions to reduce pressure, increase drainage, and to provide pain relief.

Hypothyroidism

This condition is very common in dogs and it can produce a wide variety of symptoms. Hypothyroidism occurs when the thyroid gland fails to produce enough thyroid hormone – this often leads to weigh loss as well as hair and skin problems. Fortunately, this condition is easy to diagnose with a blood test that checks the dog's levels of certain thyroid hormones like T4.

The thyroid is a gland located in your dog's neck close to the voice box, or larynx. The activity of the thyroid is regulated by the pituitary gland in the brain which produces thyroid stimulating hormone (TSH).

Signs and Symptoms

The main symptoms of this disease include lethargy, hair loss, weight gain, excessive shedding, hyper-pigmentation of skin, slow heart rate, high blood cholesterol and anemia.

Causes and Diagnosis

Hypothyroidism occurs when the thyroid produces insufficient thyroid hormone – this is most often caused by a destruction of the thyroid gland. This is often associated with other diseases like cancer or atrophy of the thyroid tissue. The use of certain medications can affect the thyroid gland as well. Hypothyroidism is most commonly diagnosed in dogs between 4 and 10 years of age.

Treatments

Treatment usually involves daily treatment with synthetic thyroid hormone.

Von Willebrand's Disease

Von Willebrand's disease (or vWD) is a disease of the blood that affects certain dog breeds more than others. This disease is caused a deficiency of von Willebrand Factor (vWF) in the dog's blood. Von Willebrand Factor is a type of adhesive glycoprotein found in the blood which is required for normal platelet binding, or clotting.

Signs and Symptoms

Lack of vWF can lead to excessive bleeding following even a minor injury. It may also cause nosebleeds, bloody urine, bloody stool, bleeding gums, and vaginal bleeding (in females). It can also cause bruising and anemia.

Causes and Diagnosis

This disease is an inherited condition caused by genetic mutations that affect the synthesis, release and stability of vWF. In order to diagnose vWD, your veterinarian will perform a physical exam as well as a medical history. Blood count and blood chemical profiles will also be obtained along with a urinalysis and electrolyte panel.

Treatment

A transfusion with fresh plasma and fresh blood to increase the supply of vWF in the blood is the best treatment for this disease. Fortunately, this condition can be managed in mild to moderate cases. Dogs with more severe vWD may require additional transfusions for surgery and supportive care may be required following spontaneous bleeding episodes.

Intervertebral Disk Disease

Intervertebral disk disease (IVDD) is another musculoskeletal issue common in Yorkie Poos. This condition causes a wide variety of different symptoms ranging from mild pain to completely paralysis – it can also mimic the presentation of other musculoskeletal problems which can delay diagnosis. IVDD can occur in any breed, though it is more common in certain breeds including the Yorkie Poo.

Signs and Symptoms

The symptoms of IVDD are highly variable and may include neck pain or stiffness, back pain or stiffness, abdominal tenderness, arched back, lameness, sensitivity to touch, stilted gait, reluctance to rise, loss of coordination, tremors, collapse, and paralysis. These symptoms most commonly present after strenuous activity of physical trauma. The most common cause of this condition is related to a disorder of cartilage formation called chondrodystrophy and it usually presents in dogs aged 3 to 6 years old.

Treatment

There are both medical and surgical treatment options available for intervertebral disk disease. Medical treatments may involve corticosteroids or non-steroidal anti-inflammatories aimed to treat pain and control inflammation. Surgical treatments may help to decompress the spinal cord or to inject enzymes to help stabilize the affected disks.

Progressive Retinal Atrophy

Another eye problem known to affect the Yorkie Poo breed is progressive retinal atrophy, or PRA. This condition affects more than 100 different breeds and it is generally an inherited condition passed on through the genes. PRA affects the retina of the eye, the part that receives light and converts it into electrical nerve signals that the brain interprets as vision. Dogs with PRA typically experience arrested retinal development (called retina dysplasia) or early degeneration of the photoreceptors in the eye. Dogs with retinal dysplasia usually develop symptoms within 2 months and are often blind by 1 year.

Signs and Symptoms

The signs of PRA vary according to the rate of progression. This disease is not painful and it doesn't affect the outward appearance of the eye. In most cases, dog owners notice a change in the dog's willingness to go down stairs, or to go down a dark hallway – PRA causes night blindness which can progress to total blindness.

Recommended Vaccinations for Yorkie Poos

Like other dog breeds, Yorkie Poos, as healthy as they are, can still catch different bacterial and viral infections once in a while; having your Yorkie Poo vaccinated is the best way to protect him from common canine diseases like distemper and parvovirus fortunately it can be prevented through vaccination.

It is important to have your puppy vaccinated at an early age and to follow your vet's recommendations for annual booster shots. The vaccination recommendations listed below for your dog highly depends on the availability in your area, your dog's age, and any other risk factors specific to its lifestyle.

In this section you will learn the vaccination schedule that your puppy or dog may need, but be sure to consult the veterinarian for further instructions.

Vaccination Schedule for Dogs			
Vaccine	**Doses**	**Age**	**Booster**
Rabies	1	12 weeks	annual
Distemper	3	6-16 weeks	3 years
Parvovirus	3	6-16 weeks	3 years
Adenovirus	3	6-16 weeks	3 years
Parainfluenza	3	6 weeks, 12-14 weeks	3 years
Bordatella	1	6 weeks	annual
Lyme Disease	2	9, 13-14 weeks	annual
Leptospirosis	2	12 and 16 weeks	annual
Canine Influenza	2	6-8, 8-12 weeks	annual

Consult with your local veterinarian to determine the appropriate vaccination schedule for your dog. Remember, recommendations vary depending on the age, breed, and health status of the dog, the potential of the dog to be exposed to the disease, the type of vaccine, whether the dog is used for breeding, and the geographical area where the dog lives or may visit.

Signs of Possible Illnesses

- **Sneezing** - does your dog have nose discharge?
- **Dehydration** - does your dog drink less than the usual? It may be a sign that there is something wrong with your dog
- **Obesity** - is your dog showing signs of obesity? It may be prone to a heart disease, or diabetes. Monitor your dog's weight before it's too late.
- **Elimination** - does your dog regularly urinate and defecate? Always check its litter to make sure that its stool and urine is normal. Contact the vet immediately if there are any signs of bleed and diarrhea.
- **Vomiting** - does your dog vomits and is it showing signs of appetite loss?

- **Coat** - does its coat and skin still feel soft, firm and rejuvenated? If your dog is sick sometimes, it appears physically on its body.
- **Paws/Limbs** - does your dog have trouble walking or is it only dragging its legs? It could be a sign of paralysis.
- **Eyes** - are there any discharge in the eyes?
- **Overall Physique** - does your dog stays active or are there any signs of weakness and deterioration?

Yorkie Poo Care Sheet

Congratulate yourself! You are now on your way to becoming a very well-informed and pro-active Yorkie Poo dog owner! Finishing this book is a huge milestone for you and your future or present pet, but before this ultimate guide comes to a conclusion, keep in mind the most important things you have acquired through reading this book.

This chapter will outline the summary of what you have learned, including the checklist you need to keep in mind to ensure that you and your Yorkie Poo lived happily ever after!

Basic Yorkie Poo Information

Pedigree: Hybrid of Yorkshire Terrier and Miniature/Toy Poodle

Group: Not Applicable; Not recognized in American Kennel Club (AKC)

Breed Size: Small

Height: 7 – 10 inches (18 – 25 cm)

Weight: 5 to 12 pounds

Coat Length: straight, curly short coat

Coat Texture: fine, silky, smooth

Color: cream, black, white, red, sable, apricot, tan, chocolate, gray, and silver

Markings: mix markings

Ears: erect; small, triangular in shape

Temperament: loyal, confident, obedient, agile, active, social

Strangers: may be wary around strangers

Other Dogs: generally good with other dogs if properly trained and socialized

Other Pets: friendly with other pets but if not properly introduce may result to potential aggression

Training: agile, intelligent and very trainable

Exercise Needs: very active; doesn't require regular or excessive amount of exercise

Health Conditions: generally healthy but predisposed to cataracts, retinal detachment, dry eye, corneal dystrophy, keratitis, hypoglycemia, and progressive retinal atrophy

Lifespan: average 12 to 15 years

Habitat Requirements

Recommended Accessories: crate, dog bed, food/water dishes, toys, collar, leash, harness, grooming supplies

Collar and Harness: sized by weight

Grooming Supplies: soft brittle brush, nail clipper

Grooming Frequency: occasional brushing; professional grooming at least 2 times a year

Energy Level: relatively high

Exercise Requirements: at least once a day plus active playtime

Crate: highly recommended

Crate Size: just large enough for dog to lie down and turn around comfortably

Crate Extras: lined with blanket or plush pet bed

Food/Water: preferably stainless steel or ceramic bowls

Toys: start with an assortment, see what the dog likes; include some mentally stimulating toys

Training: play games to give your dog extra exercise during the day; train your dog for various dog sports

Nutritional Needs

Nutritional Needs: water, protein, carbohydrate, fats, vitamins, minerals

Calorie Needs: varies by age, weight, and activity level; RER modified with activity level

Amount to Feed (puppy): feed freely but consult recommendations on the package preferably 3 – 6 times a day.

Amount to Feed (adult): consult recommendations on the package; calculated by weight

Important Ingredients: fresh animal protein (chicken, beef, lamb, turkey, eggs), digestible carbohydrates (rice, oats, barley), animal fats

Important Minerals: calcium, phosphorus, potassium, magnesium, iron, copper and manganese

Important Vitamins: Vitamin A, Vitamin A, Vitamin B-12, Vitamin D, Vitamin C

Certifications: AAFCO statement of nutritional adequacy; protein at top of ingredients list; no artificial flavors, dyes, preservatives

Breeding Information

Age of First Heat: around 7 months (or earlier)

Heat (Estrus) Cycle: 15 to 21 days

Frequency: twice a year, every 6 to 7 months

Greatest Fertility: 11 to 15 days into the cycle

Gestation Period: 58 to 65 days

Pregnancy Detection: possible after 21 days, best to wait 28 days before exam

Feeding Pregnant Dogs: maintain normal diet until week 5 or 6 then slightly increase rations

Signs of Labor: body temperature drops below normal 100° to 102°F (37.7° to 38.8°C), may be as low as 98°F (36.6°C); dog begins nesting in a dark, quiet place

Contractions: period of 10 minutes in waves of 3 to 5 followed by a period of rest

Whelping: puppies are born in 1/2 hour increments following 10 to 30 minutes of forceful straining

Puppies: born with eyes and ears closed; eyes open at 3 weeks, teeth develop at 10 weeks

Litter Size: average 6 to 10 puppies

Size at Birth: about 4.5 ounces or more

Weaning: start offering puppy food soaked in water at 6 weeks; fully weaned by 8 weeks

Socialization: start as early as possible to prevent puppies from being nervous as an adult

Index

A

AAFCO 58, 116, 128
accessories 49
active 14, 114
Adenovirus 108
adopting 2, 36
age 6, 11, 19, 20, 42, 58, 82, 88, 98, 99, 100, 103, 107, 115
alpha dog 67
American Kennel Club 3
antibodies 87
appearance 1, 3, 4, 5, 107
award 3

B

barking 48
bathing 73, 74, 75, 77
bed 49, 50, 115
behavior 4, 41, 68, 69, 71, 78, 83, 85
bitch 4, 5
bleeding 79, 104, 105
body 5, 6, 41
Bordatella 108
bowls 50, 52, 115
breed 1, 2, 4, 5, 6, 10, 12, 19, 21, 29, 30, 34, 35, 36, 48, 50, 57, 61, 82, 83, 84, 85, 101, 105, 106
breeder 22, 24, 34, 35, 36, 37, 42, 129
breeding 2, 5, 6, 34, 35, 77, 78, 82, 84, 85
brush 5
brushing 30, 74, 75, 77, 78

C

cage 4
cancer 82, 103
Canine Influenza 108
carbohydrates 55, 59, 116
care..3
carrier 49
castrate..5
cause.. 76, 79, 98, 104, 106
chewing 48, 51
children..2, 11, 13, 66, 113
clicker training..67
coat.. 4, 5, 6, 7, 10, 13, 30, 51, 56, 73, 75, 76, 77, 113
collar 18, 28, 51, 114
color...5, 6, 10, 13, 66, 113
coloration 6
coloring..4
colors 6, 10, 60
colostrum 87
comb..5, 51, 74, 75
command 5
conception..84, 85
condition 5, 73
contractions 86, 87
coordination..100, 105
costs..28, 82, 128, 130
crate.. 22, 47, 49, 50, 52, 70, 71, 72, 114

D

dam..4, 6
Degenerative Myelopathy 100
diagnosis..98, 100, 105
diet.. 2, 55, 56, 57, 85, 116, 129, 131
discharge 83
disease................................19, 22, 78, 98, 100, 103, 104, 105, 106, 107
disorder 5
distemper 107

Distemper..108
dog bed..114
dog training 67, 69
double coat 4

E

ear4, 6
ears 5, 10, 13, 73, 76, 77, 78, 88, 113, 117
eating...7, 41, 43
energy...12, 56, 60
Epilepsy 97
estrus cycle..82, 85
exercise...12, 47, 48, 99, 115
expense 19
eye 3
eye problems...12
eyes.. 3, 10, 44, 76, 77, 88, 117

F

face 3
fats.. 55, 56, 59, 115, 116
feeding.. 60, 61, 70, 85, 88, 130
female..3, 4, 5, 6
food 7, 28, 43, 49, 52, 55, 57, 58, 59, 60, 61, 66, 71, 82, 88, 114, 117
foot 6

G

games 48, 115
gene 3
genealogy 6
genetic...5
gestation period..84, 85
Glaucoma 101, 102
grooming 12, 28, 74, 75, 77, 78, 114
growth 6

H

habitat 2, 48

hair 3, 4, 5, 6

harness 114

health 2, 4, 27, 34, 51, 56, 57, 73, 78, 98, 130

health problems 2, 34, 78

healthy 128

heart disease 78

heat 77, 82, 83

herding 114

hip5

Hip Dysplasia 5, 98

history 104

hormone 102, 103

house 3, 4

housetraining 22, 49, 69, 71

housing 82

Hypothyroidism 102, 103

I

illness 41

ingredients 55, 58, 59, 60, 116

intelligent 11, 14, 30, 67, 114

Intervertebral Disk Disease 105

K

kennel 4

L

labor 86, 87

leash 49, 51, 83, 114

legs 5, 76

Leptospirosis 108

license 17, 18, 28, 51

licensing 17
lifespan 12
litter 7, 33, 36, 41, 82, 84, 86
longhaired 74

M

markings 6
milk 7
minerals 55, 57, 115
money 19, 82
musculoskeletal 98, 105
mutation 100

N

nails 73, 77, 79
nose 10, 76
nursing 87, 88
nutrients 55, 87, 130
nutritional needs 58

O

obedience 37
obesity 60
outer coat 7

P

pain 99, 100, 102, 105, 106
Parainfluenza 108
paralysis 101, 105, 106
parent 4, 6
Parvovirus 108
pet store 34
pets 11, 14, 30, 78, 114, 128

positive reinforcement 67, 68

pregnant...82, 84

Progressive Retinal Atrophy 106

pros and cons 29

protein.. 55, 56, 58, 59, 60, 85, 115, 116

punishment 67, 68

pupil...102

puppies..5, 7, 8, 42

puppy..... 2, 22, 24, 28, 33, 34, 35, 36, 41, 42, 43, 44, 50, 52, 61, 65, 67, 69, 70, 71, 72, 87,
    88, 107, 115, 117, 128, 129, 130

puppy mills 34, 37

puppy-proofing 33, 130

purebred...3, 37

Q

quick 79

R

rabies..18, 19

record 6

registry...3

rescue 36

reward 67, 68, 71, 78

S

seizures...97, 98

shed 75

show 3

showing 2

signs...41

sire 4, 6

size.. 12, 20, 22, 50, 51, 61, 84

skin...................................... 4, 6, 27, 51, 56, 66, 73, 75, 76, 102, 103

skull..3

socialization...11, 65, 69 spay..5

stimulation 12, 48

supplies... 44, 49, 52, 74, 75, 79, 114

surgery...6, 105

symptoms 99, 101, 102, 103, 105, 107

T

tail4, 5, 76

teeth 3, 73, 77, 78, 117

temperament 1

temperature..86, 117

thyroid gland 102, 103

tips 33, 36, 47, 52, 129

toxic 44, 61

toys 28, 43, 48, 50, 52, 114, 115

train 115

training 11, 37, 67, 68, 69, 70

treatment 2, 101, 102, 103, 106

treats 27, 66

trim 5

trimming...4

types 47, 82

U

undercoat 4

undercoat rake..51, 75

urine marking...83

uterus 84, 85

V

vaccination 18

veterinarian... 28, 61, 85, 87, 100, 104

vitamins 55, 56, 115, 131

von Willebrand Factor 104

Von Willebrand's Disease 104

vulva 83

W

water 44, 49, 50, 52, 57, 59, 71, 76, 88, 114, 115, 117
weaned...43
weight.. 60, 85, 98, 103, 114, 115
whelping..86, 88
whelping box...86
wire pin brush 51, 75

Photo Credits

Page 1 Photo By dren88 via Flickr.com,
<https://www.flickr.com/photos/robwiss/4637143711/>

Page 9 Photo By Isaac Singleton via Flickr.com,
<https://www.flickr.com/photos/isaacsingleton/4415295753/>

Page 16 Photo By petmutt via Flickr.com,
<https://www.flickr.com/photos/76741766@N00/5381874996/>

Page 33 Photo By vv@ldzen via Flickr.com,
<https://www.flickr.com/photos/46157135@N06/4464077590/>

Page 46 Photo By petmutt via Flickr.com,
<https://www.flickr.com/photos/76741766@N00/5381874996/in/photolist>

Page 53 Photo By Jennifer Aitkens via Flickr.com,
<https://www.flickr.com/photos/molajen/24932426983/>

Page 63 Photo By petmutt via Flickr.com,
<https://www.flickr.com/photos/76741766@N00/5484227814/in/photostream/>

Page 72 Photo By James Marvin Phelps via Flickr.com, <https://www.flickr.com/photos/mandj98/14182669771/>

Page 80 Photo By petmutt via Flickr.com, <https://www.flickr.com/photos/76741766@N00/5280426945/in/photostream/>

Page 89 Photo By Jennifer Aitkens via Flickr.com, <https://www.flickr.com/photos/molajen/5612172406/in/photostream/>

Page 110 Photo By star5112 via Flickr.com, <https://www.flickr.com/photos/johnjoh/177566576/>

References

"AAFCO Dog Food Nutrient Profiles"
DogFoodAdvisor.com
<http://www.dogfoodadvisor.com/frequently-asked-questions/aafco-nutrient-profiles/>

"Annual Dog Care Costs" PetFinder.com
<https://www.petfinder.com/pet-adoption/dog-adoption/annual-dog-care-costs/>

"Choosing a Healthy Puppy" WebMD
<http://pets.webmd.com/dogs/guide/choosing-healthy-puppy>

"How to Find a Responsible Breeder" HumaneSociety.org
<http://www.humanesociety.org/issues/puppy_mills/tips/finding_responsible_dog_breeder.html?referrer=https://www.google.com/>

"My Bowl: What Goes into a Balanced Diet for Your Dog?" PetMD.com
<http://www.petmd.com/dog/slideshows/nutrition-center/my-bowl-what-goes-into-a-balanced-diet-for-your-dog>

"Nutrients Your Dog Needs" ASPCA.org
<https://www.aspca.org/pet-care/dog-care/nutrients-your-dog-needs>

"Nutrition: General Feeding Guidelines for Dogs"
VCAAnimalHospitals.com
<http://www.vcahospitals.com/main/pet-health-information/article/animal-health/nutrition-general-feeding-guidelines-for-dogs/6491>

"Pet Care Costs" ASPCA.org
<https://www.aspca.org/adopt/pet-care-costs>

"Puppy Proofing Your Home" Hill's Pet.com
<http://www.hillspet.com/dog-care/puppy-proofing-your-home.html>

"Puppy Proofing Your Home" PetEducation.com
<http://www.peteducation.com/article.cfm?c=2+2106&aid=3283>

"The Yorkie Poo" AKC.org
<http://www.akc.org/dog-breeds/cane-corso/>

"Vitamins and Minerals Your Dog Needs" Kim Boatman
TheDogDaily.com
<http://www.thedogdaily.com/dish/diet/dogs_vitamins/inde
x.html#.VHOtMPnF_IA>

"YorkiePoo" AKC.org
<http://www.akc.org/dog-owners/canine-
partners/spotlight/yorkiepoo/>

"Yorkie-Poo" PetGuide.com
<http://www.petguide.com/breeds/dog/yorkie-poo/>

**"Yorkiepoo Dog Breed Information, Pictures,
Characteristics and Facts"** PetBreeds.com
<http://dogs.petbreeds.com/l/218/Yorkiepoo>

"Yorkie Poo Health Problems" Naomi Millburn, Demand
Media – TheNest.com
<http://pets.thenest.com/yorkie-poo-health-problems-
12676.html>

"Yorkie Poo Information" GreatDogSite.com
<http://www.greatdogsite.com/hybrids/details/Yorkie_Poo/>

**"Yorkie Poo Information: Interesting Facts about
Yorkiedoodles"** Debra Pope – YorkiePooInformation.net
<http://www.yorkiepooinformation.net/>

"Yorkie Poo Information: Personality and Facts"
<http://maacobowllv.com/yorkie-poo-information-personality-and-facts/>

"Yorkipoo: Yorkshire Terrier / Poodle Hybrid Dogs Information and Pictures" DogBreedInfo.com
<http://www.dogbreedinfo.com/yorkipoo.htm>

Feeding Baby
Cynthia Cherry
978-1941070000

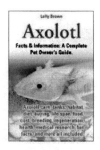

Axolotl
Lolly Brown
978-0989658430

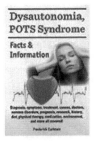

Dysautonomia, POTS
Syndrome
Frederick Earlstein
978-0989658485

Degenerative Disc
Disease Explained
Frederick Earlstein
978-0989658485

Sinusitis, Hay Fever,
Allergic Rhinitis Explained
Frederick Earlstein
978-1941070024

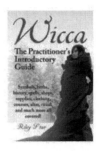

Wicca
Riley Star
978-1941070130

Zombie Apocalypse
Rex Cutty
978-1941070154

Capybara
Lolly Brown
978-1941070062

Eels As Pets
Lolly Brown
978-1941070167

Scabies and Lice Explained
Frederick Earlstein
978-1941070017

Saltwater Fish As Pets
Lolly Brown
978-0989658461

Torticollis Explained
Frederick Earlstein
978-1941070055

Kennel Cough
Lolly Brown
978-0989658409

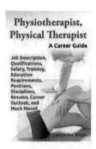

Physiotherapist, Physical
Therapist
Christopher Wright
978-0989658492

Rats, Mice, and Dormice
As Pets
Lolly Brown
978-1941070079

Wallaby and Wallaroo Care
Lolly Brown
978-1941070031

Bodybuilding Supplements
Explained
Jon Shelton
978-1941070239

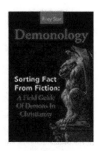

Demonology
Riley Star
978-19401070314

Pigeon Racing
Lolly Brown
978-1941070307

Dwarf Hamster
Lolly Brown
978-1941070390

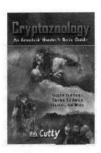

Cryptozoology
Rex Cutty
978-1941070406

Eye Strain
Frederick Earlstein
978-1941070369

Inez The Miniature Elephant
Asher Ray
978-1941070353

Vampire Apocalypse
Rex Cutty
978-1941070321

Made in the USA
Columbia, SC
28 November 2020

25731326R00080